# The Lion Book
# of Humorous Verse

Here's verse——
That's not alphabetical,
Nor even theoretical;
Not biographical.
Nor always ecstatical.
It has no apologies,
Or heady mythologies.
It's humour and nonsense—
Who knows what consequence?

# THE
# LION BOOK OF
# HUMOROUS
# VERSE

Chosen by Ruth Petrie

**COLLINS·LIONS**

First published in Lions 1972
by William Collins Sons & Co Ltd
14 St James's Place, London SW1
Sixth Impression February 1979

Made and printed in Great Britain by
William Collins Sons & Co Ltd, Glasgow

# Contents

# Limericks of Edward Lear

There was an Old Person whose habits
Induced him to feed upon Rabbits;
   When he'd eaten eighteen,
   He turned perfectly green,
Upon which he relinquished those habits.

There was an Old Man on a hill,
Who seldom, if ever, stood still;
   He ran up and down,
   In his Grandmother's gown,
Which adorned that Old Man on a hill.

# Limericks of Edward Lear

There was an Old Lady of Chertsey,
Who made a remarkable curtsey;
    She twirled round and round,
    Till she sunk underground,
Which distressed all the people of Chertsey.

There was an Old Person of Gretna,
Who rushed down the crater of Etna;
    When they said, 'Is it hot?'
    He replied, 'No, it's not!'
That mendacious Old Person of Gretna.

# Growltiger's Last Stand

Growltiger was a Bravo Cat, who lived upon a barge:
In fact he was the roughest cat that ever roamed at
   large.
From Gravesend up to Oxford he pursued his evil
   aims,
Rejoicing in his title of 'The Terror of the Thames'.


His manners and appearance did not calculate to
   please;
His coat was torn and seedy, he was baggy at the
   knees;
One ear was somewhat missing, no need to tell you
   why,
And he scowled upon a hostile world from one
   forbidding eye.


The cottagers of Rotherhithe knew something of his
   fame,
At Hammersmith and Putney people shuddered at
   his name.
They would fortify the hen-house, lock up the silly
   goose,
When the rumour ran along the shore: GROWL-
   TIGER'S ON THE LOOSE!


Woe to the weak canary, that fluttered from its cage;
Woe to the pampered Pekinese, that faced Growl-
   tiger's rage.

Woe to the bristly Bandicoot, that lurks on foreign
ships,
And woe to any Cat with whom Growltiger came to
grips!


But most to Cats of foreign race his hatred had been
vowed;
To Cats of foreign name and race no quarter was
allowed.
The Persian and the Siamese regarded him with
fear—
Because it was a Siamese had mauled his missing ear.


Now on a peaceful summer night, all nature seemed
at play,
The tender moon was shining bright, the barge at
Molesey lay.
All in the balmy moonlight it lay rocking on the
tide—
And Growltiger was disposed to show his sentimental
side.


His bucko mate, GRUMBUSKIN, long since had dis-
appeared,
For to the Bell at Hampton he had gone to wet his
beard;
And his bosun, TUMBLEBRUTUS, he too had stol'n
away—
In the yard behind the Lion he was prowling for his
prey.

In the forepeak of the vessel Growltiger sate alone,
Concentrating his attention on the Lady GRIDDLE-
    BONE.
And his raffish crew were sleeping in their barrels
    and their bunks—
As the Siamese came creeping in their sampans and
    their junks.

Growltiger had no eye or ear for aught but Griddle-
    bone,
And the Lady seemed enraptured by his manly
    baritone,
Disposed to relaxation, and awaiting no surprise—
But the moonlight shone reflected from a thousand
    bright blue eyes.

And closer still and closer the sampans circled round,
And yet from all the enemy there was not heard a
    sound.
The lovers sang their last duet, in danger of their
    lives—
For the foe was armed with toasting forks and cruel
    carving knives.

Then GILBERT gave the signal to his fierce Mon-
    golian horde;
With a frightful burst of fireworks the Chinks they
    swarmed aboard.
Abandoning their sampans and their pullaways and
    junks,
They battened down the hatches on the crew within
    their bunks.

Then Griddlebone she gave a screech, for she was
    badly skeered;
I am sorry to admit it, but she quickly disappeared.
She probably escaped with ease, I'm sure she was not
    drowned—
But a serried ring of flashing steel Growltiger did
    surround.

The ruthless foe pressed forward, in stubborn rank
    on rank;
Growltiger to his vast surprise was forced to walk the
    plank.
He who a hundred victims had driven to that drop,
At the end of all his crimes was forced to go ker-flip,
    ker-flop.

Oh there was joy in Wapping when the news flew
    through the land;
At Maidenhead and Henley there was dancing on
    the strand.
Rats were roasted whole at Brentford, and at Vic-
    toria Dock,
And a day of celebration was commanded in
    Bangkok.

*T. S. Eliot*

# Ruthless Rhymes of Harry Graham

## Opportunity

When Mrs Gorm (Aunt Eloïse)
Was stung to death by savage bees,
Her husband (Prebendary Gorm)
Put on his veil, and took the swarm.
He's publishing a book next May
On 'How to Make Bee-keeping Pay'.

## Uncle

Uncle, whose inventive brains
Kept evolving aeroplanes,
Fell from an enormous height
On my garden lawn, last night.
 Flying is a fatal sport,
 Uncle wrecked the tennis-court.

## Necessity

Late last night I slew my wife,
 Stretched her on the parquet flooring
I was loth to take her life,
 But I *had* to stop her snoring!

# Next!

I thought that I would like to see
The early world that used to be,
That mastodonic mausoleum,
The Natural History Museum.
On iron seat in marble bower,
I slumbered through the closing hour.
At midnight in the vasty hall
The fossils gathered for a ball.
High above notices and bulletins
Loomed up the Mesozoic skeletons.
Aroused by who knows what elixirs,
They ground along like concrete mixers.
They bowed and scraped in reptile pleasure,
And then began to tread the measure.
There were no drums or saxophones,
But just the clatter of their bones,
A rolling, rattling, carefree circus
Of mammoth polkas and mazurkas.
Pterodactyls and brontosauruses
Sang ghostly prehistoric choruses.
Amid the megalosauric wassail
I caught the eye of one small fossil.
Cheer up, old man, he said, and winked—
It's kind of fun to be extinct.

*Ogden Nash*

# Ermyntrude

A little girl named Ermyntrude
Was often curiously rude—
Come down to breakfast in the nude.
Her sister said (though not a prude):
'It seems to me extremely crude
To see your tummy over food:
Your conduct borders on the lewd.

Also, you nastily exude
Cornflakes and milk as though you'd spewed'—
Her lips were open when she chewed,
And read a comic-book called *Dude*.
She was a sight not to be viewed
Without profound disquietude.
Though what could come but such a mood
From anyone named Ermyntrude?

*Roy Fuller*


# The Man of Thessaly

There was a Man of Thessaly,
    And he was wondrous wise:
He jumped into a briar hedge
    And scratched out both his eyes.
But when he saw his eyes were out,
    With all his might and main
He jumped into another hedge
    And scratched them in again.

*Anon*

# The Python

A Python I should not advise,—
It needs a doctor for its eyes,
And has the measles yearly.

However, if you feel inclined
To get one (to improve your mind,
And not from fashion merely),
Allow no music near its cage;

And when it flies into a rage
Chastise it, most severely.

I had an aunt in Yucatan
Who bought a Python from a man
    And kept it for a pet.
She died, because she never knew
These simple little rules and few;—

The Snake is living yet.
*H. Belloc*

# The March to Moscow

The Emperor Nap he would set off
  On a summer excursion to Moscow;
The fields were green and the sky was blue,
    Morbleu! Parbleu!
  What a splendid excursion to Moscow!


The Emperor Nap he talk'd so big
  That he frighten'd Mr Roscoe.
And Counsellor Brougham was all in a fume
  At the thought of the march to Moscow:
The Russians, he said, they were undone,
    And the great Fee-Faw-Fum
    Would presently come,
With a hop, step, and jump, unto London,
  For, as for his conquering Russia,
  However some persons might scoff it,
  Do it he could, do it he would,
And from doing it nothing would come but good,
  And nothing would call him off it.


But the Russians stoutly they turned to
  Upon the road to Moscow.
Nap had to fight his way all through;
They could fight, though they could not parlez-vous;
But the fields were green, and the sky was blue,
    Morbleu! Parbleu!
  And so he got to Moscow.

He found the place too warm for him,
    For they set fire to Moscow.
To get there had cost him much ado,
And then no better course he knew
While the fields were green, and the sky was blue,
        Morbleu! Parbleu!
But to march back again from Moscow.

The Russians they stuck close to him
    All on the road from Moscow—
And Shouvaloff he shovell'd them off,
And Markoff he mark'd them off,
And Krosnoff he cross'd them off,
And Touchkoff he touch'd them off,
And Boroskoff he bored them off,
And Kutousoff he cut them off,
And Parenzoff he pared them off,
And Worronzoff he worried them off,
And Doctoroff he doctor'd them off,
And Rodinoff he flogg'd them off.
And, last of all, an Admiral came,
A terrible man with a terrible name,
A name which you all know by sight very well,
But which no one can speak, and no one can spell.

And then came on the frost and snow
    All on the road from Moscow.
Worse and worse every day the elements grew,
The fields were so white and the sky was so blue,
        Sacrebleu! Ventrebleu!
What a horrible journey from Moscow.

24

Too cold upon the road was he;
Too hot he had been at Moscow;
But colder and hotter he may be,
For the grave is colder than Muscovy;
And a place there is to be kept in view,
Where the fire is red, and the brimstone blue,
      Morbleu! Parbleu!
But there he must stay for a very long day,
For from thence there is no stealing away,
   As there was on the road from Moscow.

*Robert Southey*

# On Dr Isaac Letsome

When people's ill they comes to I,
   I physics, bleeds, and sweats 'em,
Sometimes they live, sometimes they die;
   What's that to I? I Letsome.

*Anon*

# The Sad Demise of Sally Point-Toe Jane

They ought to have known much better—
The Mrs Black and ffrencham-fist—
When they added the name Sally Point-Toe Jane
To their Dance Invitation List.


They *could* have said, 'Dear Sally,
There are buns and jellics galore.
Eat your fill, but promise you will stay over here
    with Jackie and Jill
Away from the ballroom floor.'


Sally Jane would have stayed where they'd told her,
She generally did what they said,
But the band struck up for a waltz
And the music went straight to her head.


Before they could shout 'Come back here!'
While they shrieked and stamped and swore,
Sally Point-Toe Jane, as true as her name, stood up
    and twirled, and twirled again,
And drilled herself right through the floor.

*Grimsdyke Churchforest*

# How Pleasant to Know Mr Lear

How pleasant to know Mr Lear!
  Who has written such volumes of stuff!
Some think him ill-tempered and queer,
  But a few think him pleasant enough.

His mind is concrete and fastidious,
  His nose is remarkably big;
His visage is more or less hideous,
  His beard it resembles a wig.

He has ears, and two eyes, and ten fingers,
  Leastways if you reckon two thumbs;
Long ago he was one of the singers,
  But now he is one of the dumbs.

He sits in a beautiful parlour,
  With hundreds of books on the wall;
He drinks a great deal of Marsala,
  But never gets tipsy at all.

He has many friends, laymen and clerical;
  Old Foss is the name of his cat;
His body is perfectly spherical,
  He weareth a runcible hat.

When he walks in a waterproof white,
  The children run after him so!
Calling out, 'He's come out in his night-
  Gown, that crazy old Englishman, oh!'

He weeps by the side of the ocean,
  He weeps on the top of the hill;
He purchases pancakes and lotion,
  And chocolate shrimps from the mill.

He reads but he cannot speak Spanish,
  He cannot abide ginger-beer:
Ere the days of his pilgrimage vanish,
  How pleasant to know Mr Lear!

*Edward Lear*

# Incidents in the Life of My Uncle Arly

### I

O My agèd Uncle Arly!
Sitting on a heap of Barley
   Thro' the silent hours of night,—
Close beside a leafy thicket:—
On his nose there was a Cricket,—
In his hat a Railway Ticket;—
   (But his shoes were far too tight.)

### II

Long ago, in youth, he squander'd
All his goods away, and wander'd
   To the Tiniskoop-hills afar.
There on golden sunsets blazing,
Every evening found him gazing,—
Singing,—'Orb! you're quite amazing!
   'How I wonder what you are!'

### III

Like the ancient Medes and Persians,
Always by his own exertions
   He subsisted on those hills;—
Whiles,—by teaching children spelling,—
Or at times by merely yelling,—
Or at intervals by selling
   Propter's Nicodemus Pills.

### IV

Later, in his morning rambles
He perceived the moving brambles—
   Something square and white disclose;—

'Twas a First-class Railway-Ticket;
But, on stooping down to pick it
Off the ground,—a pea-green Cricket
  Settled on my uncle's Nose.

### V

Never—never more,—oh! never,
Did that Cricket leave him ever,—
  Dawn or evening, day or night;—
Clinging as a constant treasure,—
Chirping with a cheerious measure,—
Wholly to my uncle's pleasure,—
  (Though his shoes were far too tight.)

### VI

So for three-and-forty winters,
Till his shoes were worn to splinters,
  All those hills he wander'd o'er,—
Sometimes silent;—sometimes yelling;—
Till he came to Borley-Melling,
Near his old ancestral dwelling;—
  (But his shoes were far too tight.)

### VII

On a little heap of barley
Died my agèd Uncle Arly,
  And they buried him one night;—
Close beside the leafy thicket;—
There,—his hat and Railway-Ticket;—
There,—his ever-faithful Cricket;—
  (But his shoes were far too tight.)

*Edward Lear*

# nobody loses all the time

i had an uncle named
Sol who was a born failure and
nearly everybody said he should have gone
into vaudeville perhaps because my Uncle Sol could
sing McCann He Was A Diver on Xmas Eve like
  Hell Itself which
may or may not account for the fact that my Uncle

Sol indulged in that possibly most inexcusable
of all to use a highfalootin phrase
luxuries that is or to
wit farming and be
it needlessly
added

my Uncle Sol's farm
failed because the chickens
ate the vegetables so
my Uncle Sol had a
chicken farm till the
skunks ate the chickens when

my Uncle Sol
had a skunk farm but
the skunks caught cold and
died and so
my Uncle Sol imitated the
skunks in a subtle manner

or by drowning himself in the watertank
but somebody who'd given my Uncle Sol a Victor

Victrola and records while he lived presented to
him upon the auspicious occasion of his decease **a**
scrumptious not to mention splendiferous funeral
    with
tall boys in black gloves and flowers and everything
    and

i remember we all cried like the Missouri
when my Uncle Sol's coffin lurched because
somebody pressed a button
(and down went
my Uncle
Sol

and started a worm farm)

                        *e e cummings*

## Epitaph on a 'Marf'

Wot a marf' e'd got,
Wot a marf.
When 'e wos a kid,
Goo' Lor' luv'll
'Is pore old muvver
Must 'a' fed 'im wiv a shuvvle.

Wot a gap 'e'd got,
Pore chap,
'E'd never been known to larf,
'Cos if 'e did
It's a penny to a quid
'E'd 'a' split 'is fice in 'arf.

                        *Traditional*

# The White Knight's Song

I'll tell thee everything I can;
   There's little to relate.
I saw an aged aged man,
   A-sitting on a gate.
'Who are you, aged man?' I said.
   'And how is it you live?'
And his answer trickled through my head
   Like water through a sieve.

He said 'I look for butterflies
   That sleep among the wheat:
I make them into mutton-pies,
   And sell them in the street.
I sell them unto men,' he said,
   'Who sail on stormy seas;
And that's the way I get my bread—
   A trifle, if you please.'

But I was thinking of a plan
   To dye one's whiskers green,
And always use so large a fan
   That they could not be seen.
So, having no reply to give
   To what the old man said,
I cried 'Come, tell me how you live!'
   And thumped him on the head.

His accents mild took up the tale:
   He said 'I go my ways,
And when I find a mountain-rill,
   I set it in a blaze;

And thence they make a stuff they call
    Rowland's Macassar-Oil—
Yet twopence-halfpenny is all
    They give me for my toil.'


But I was thinking of a way
    To feed oneself on batter,
And so go on from day to day
    Getting a little fatter.
I shook him well from side to side,
    Until his face was blue:
'Come, tell me how you live,' I cried,
    'And what it is you do!'


He said 'I hunt for haddocks' eyes
    Among the heather bright,
And work them into waistcoat-buttons
    In the silent night.
And these I do not sell for gold
    Or coin of silvery shine,
But for a copper halfpenny,
    And that will purchase nine.


'I sometimes dig for buttered rolls,
    Or set limed twigs for crabs;
I sometimes search the grassy knolls
    For wheels of Hansom-cabs.
And that's the way' (he gave a wink)
    'By which I get my wealth—
And very gladly will I drink
    Your Honour's noble health.'

I heard him then, for I had just
   Completed my design
To keep the Menai bridge from rust
   By boiling it in wine.
I thanked him much for telling me
   The way he got his wealth,
But chiefly for his wish that he
   Might drink my noble health.

And now, if e'er by chance I put
   My fingers into glue,
Or madly squeeze a right-hand foot
   Into a left-hand shoe,
Or if I drop upon my toe
   A very heavy weight,
I weep, for it reminds me so
Of that old man I used to know—
Whose look was mild, whose speech was slow,
Whose hair was whiter than the snow,
Whose face was very like a crow,
With eyes, like cinders, all aglow,
Who seemed distracted with his woe,
Who rocked his body to and fro,
And muttered mumblingly and low,
As if his mouth were full of dough,
Who snorted like a buffalo—
That summer evening long ago
   A-sitting on a gate.

                        *Lewis Carroll*

# There was an old woman

There was an old woman who swallowed a fly;
I wonder why
She swallowed a fly.
Poor old woman, she's sure to die.

There was an old woman who swallowed a spider;
That wriggled and jiggled and wriggled inside her;
She swallowed the spider to catch the fly,
I wonder why
She swallowed a fly.
Poor old woman, she's sure to die.

There was an old woman who swallowed a bird;
How absurd
To swallow a bird.
She swallowed the bird to catch the spider,
That wriggled and jiggled and wriggled inside her.
She swallowed the spider to catch the fly,
I wonder why
She swallowed a fly.
Poor old woman, she's sure to die.

There was an old woman who swallowed a cat;
Fancy that!
She swallowed a cat;
She swallowed the cat to catch the bird,
She swallowed the bird to catch the spider,
That wriggled and jiggled and wriggled inside her.

She swallowed the spider to catch the fly,
I wonder why
She swallowed a fly.
Poor old woman, she's sure to die.

There was an old woman who swallowed a dog;
She went the whole hog
And swallowed a dog;
She swallowed the dog to catch the cat,
She swallowed the cat to catch the bird,
She swallowed the bird to catch the spider,
That wriggled and jiggled and wriggled inside her.
She swallowed the spider to catch the fly,
I wonder why
She swallowed a fly.
Poor old woman, she's sure to die.

There was an old woman who swallowed a cow;
I wonder how
She swallowed a cow;
She swallowed the cow to catch the dog,
She swallowed the dog to catch the cat,
She swallowed the cat to catch the bird,
She swallowed the bird to catch the spider,
That wriggled and jiggled and wriggled inside her.
She swallowed the spider to catch the fly,
I wonder why
She swallowed a fly.
Poor old woman, she's sure to die.

There was an old woman who swallowed a horse;
She died of course!

*Traditional English and American*

# Anonymous Limericks

There was an old party of Lyme
Who married three wives at one time.
    When asked: 'Why the third?'
    He replied, 'One's absurd,
And bigamy, sir, is a crime.'


There was a young man of Quebec
Who was frozen in snow to his neck,
    When asked, 'Are you friz?'
    He replied, 'Yes, I is,
But we don't call this cold in Quebec.'


There was a young girl, a sweet lamb,
Who smiled as she entered a tram.
    After she had embarked
    The conductor remarked,
'Your fare!' And she said, 'Yes, I am.'


There was a young man of Japan
Whose limericks never would scan;
    When they said it was so,
    He replied, 'Yes, I know,
But I always try to get as many words into the
        last line as ever I possibly can.'

# The Big Baboon

The Big Baboon is found upon
  The plains of Cariboo:

He goes about

with nothing on
(A shocking thing to do).

But if he

dressed respectably
And let his whiskers grow,

How like this Big Baboon would be

To Mister So-and-so!

*H. Belloc*

# Etiquette

The *Ballyshannon* foundered off the coast of Cariboo,
And down in fathoms many went the captain and
the crew;
Down went the owners—greedy men whom hope of
gain allured:
Oh, dry the starting tear, for they were heavily
insured.

Besides the captain and the mate, the owners and the
crew,
The passengers were also drowned excepting only
two;
Young Peter Gray, who tasted teas for Baker, Croop,
and Co.,
And Somers, who from Eastern shores imported
indigo.

These passengers, by reason of their clinging to a
mast,
Upon a desert island were eventually cast.
They hunted for their meals, as Alexander Selkirk
used,
But they could not chat together—they had not been
introduced.

For Peter Gray, and Somers too, though certainly in
trade,
Were properly particular about the friends they
made;

And somehow thus they settled it without a word of
mouth—
That Gray should take the northern half, while
Somers took the south.

On Peter's portion oysters grew—a delicacy rare,
But oysters were a delicacy Peter couldn't bear.
On Somers' side was turtle, on the shingle lying thick
Which Somers couldn't eat, because it always made
him sick.

Gray gnashed his teeth with envy as he saw a mighty
store
Of turtle unmolested on his fellow-creature's shore:
The oysters at his feet aside impatiently he shoved,
For turtle and his mother were the only things he
loved.

And Somers sighed in sorrow as he settled in the
south,
For the thought of Peter's oysters brought the water
to his mouth.
He longed to lay him down upon the shelly bed, and
stuff:
He had often eaten oysters, but had never had
enough.

How they wished an introduction to each other
they had had
When on board the *Ballyshannon*! And it drove them
nearly mad.

To think how very friendly with each other they
    might get,
If it wasn't for the arbitrary rule of etiquette!

One day, when out a-hunting for the *mus ridiculus*,
Gray overheard his fellow-man soliloquizing thus:
'I wonder how the playmates of my youth are getting
    on,
M'Connel, S. B. Walters, Paddy Byles, and Robin-
    son?'

These simple words made Peter as delighted as could
    be,
Old Chummies at the Charterhouse were Robinson
    and he!
He walked straight up to Somers, then he turned
    extremely red,
Hesitated, hummed and hawed a bit, then cleared
    his throat and said:

'I beg your pardon—pray forgive me if I seem too
    bold,
But you have breathed a name I knew familiarly of
    old.
You spoke aloud of Robinson—I happened to be
    by—
You know him?' 'Yes, extremely well.' 'Allow me—
    so do I.'

It was enough: they felt they could more sociably
    get on,

For (ah, the magic of the fact!) they each knew
    Robinson!
And Mr Somers' turtle was at Peter's service quite,
And Mr Somers punished Peter's oyster-beds all
    night.

They soon became like brothers from community of
    wrongs;
They wrote each other little odes and sang each other
    songs;
They told each other anecdotes disparaging their
    wives;
On several occasions, too, they saved each other's
    lives.

They felt quite melancholy when they parted for the
    night,
And got up in the morning soon as ever it was light;
Each other's pleasant company they so relied upon,
And all because it happened that they both knew
    Robinson!

They lived for many years on that inhospitable shore,
And day by day they learned to love each other more
    and more.
At last, to their astonishment, on getting up one day,
They saw a vessel anchored in the offing of the bay!

To Peter an idea occurred. 'Suppose we cross the
    main?
So good an opportunity may not occur again.'

And Somers thought a minute, then ejaculated,
    'Done!
I wonder how my business in the City's getting on?'

'But stay,' said Mr Peter: 'when in England, as you
    know,
I earned a living tasting teas for Baker, Croop, and
    Co.
I may be superseded, my employers think me dead!'
'Then come with me,' said Somers, 'and taste indigo
    instead.'

But all their plans were scattered in a moment when
    they found
The vessel was a convict ship from Portland, outward
    bound!
When a boat came off to fetch them, though they
    felt it very kind
To go on board they firmly but respectfully declined.

As both the happy settlers roared with laughter at
    the joke,
They recognized an unattractive fellow pulling
    stroke:
'Twas Robinson—a convict, in an unbecoming
    frock!
Condemned to seven years for misappropriating
    stock!!!

They laughed no more, for Somers thought he had
    been rather rash

In knowing one whose friend had misappropriated
　　cash;
And Peter thought a foolish tack he must have gone
　　upon,
In making the acquaintance of a friend of Robinson.

At first they didn't quarrel very openly, I've heard;
They nodded when they met, and now and then
　　exchanged a word:
The word grew rare, and rarer still the nodding of
　　the head,
And when they meet each other now, they cut each
　　other dead.

To allocate the island they agreed by word of mouth,
And Peter takes the north again, and Somers takes
　　the south:
And Peter has the oysters, which he loathes with
　　horror grim,
And Somers has the turtle—turtle disagrees with him.
*Sir W. S. Gilbert*


# The Terns

Said the mother Tern
　　to her baby Tern
Would you like a brother?
Said baby Tern
　　to mother Tern
Yes
One good Tern deserves another.
*Spike Milligan*

# Epitaphs—of a Sort

Although the Borgias
Were rather gorgeous
They liked the absurder
Kind of murder.

*Louis Untermeyer*


Poor Martha Snell, she's gone away
She would if she could but she could not stay
She'd two bad legs and baddish cough
But her legs it was that carried her off.

*Anon*


Here lies John Bun,
He was killed by a gun,
His name was not Bun, but Wood,
But Wood would not rhyme with gun, but Bun
would.

*Anon*


This spot is the sweetest I've seen in my life
For it raises my flowers and covers my wife.

*Anon*

# Inhuman Henry
## or
## Cruelty to Fabulous Animals

Oh would you know why Henry sleeps,
And why his mourning Mother weeps,
And why his weeping Mother mourns?
He was unkind to unicorns.

No unicorn, with Henry's leave,
Could dance upon the lawn at eve,
Or gore the gardener's boy in spring
Or do the very slightest thing.

No unicorn could safely roar,
And dash its nose against the door,
Nor sit in peace upon the mat
To eat the dog, or drink the cat.

Henry would never in the least
Encourage the heraldic beast:
If there were unicorns about
He went and let the lion out.

The lion, leaping from its chain
And glaring through its tangled mane,
Would stand on end and bark and bound
And bite what unicorns it found.

And when the lion bit a lot
Was Henry sorry? He was not.

What did his jumps betoken? Joy.
He was a bloody-minded boy.

The Unicorn is not a Goose,
And when they saw the lion loose
They grew increasingly aware
That they had better not be there.

And oh, the unicorn is fleet
And spurns the earth with all its feet.
The lion had to snap and snatch
At tips of tails it could not catch.

Returning home in temper bad,
It met the sanguinary lad,
And clasping Henry with its claws
It took his legs between its jaws.

'Down, lion, down!' said Henry, 'cease!
My legs immediately release.'
His formidable feline pet
Made no reply, but only ate.

The last words that were ever said
By Henry's disappearing head,
In accents of indignant scorn,
Were 'I am not a unicorn.'

And now you know why Henry sleeps,
And why his mother mourns and weeps,
And why she also weeps and mourns;
So now be kind to unicorns.

A. E. Housman

# Hunter Trials

It's awf'lly bad luck on Diana,
　　Her ponies have swallowed their bits;
She fished down their throats with a spanner
　　And frightened them all into fits.

So now she's attempting to borrow.
　　*Do* lend her some bits, Mummy, *do*;
I'll lend her my own for to-morrow,
　　But to-day *I*'ll be wanting them too.

Just look at Prunella on Guzzle,
　　The wizardest pony on earth;
Why doesn't she slacken his muzzle
　　And tighten the breech in his girth?

I say, Mummy, there's Mrs Geyser
　　And doesn't she look pretty sick?
I bet it's because Mona Lisa
　　Was hit on the hock with a brick.

Miss Blewitt says Monica threw it,
　　But Monica says it was Joan,
And Joan's very thick with Miss Blewitt,
　　So Monica's sulking alone.

And Margaret failed in her paces,
　　Her withers got tied in a noose,
So her coronets caught in the traces
　　And now all her fetlocks are loose.

Oh, it's me now. I'm terribly nervous.
   I wonder if Smudges will shy.
She's practically certain to swerve as
   Her Pelham is over one eye.

     *     *     *     *

Oh wasn't it naughty of Smudges?
   Oh, Mummy, I'm sick with disgust,
She threw me in front of the Judges,
   And my silly old collarbone's bust.

John Betjeman

# On a Clergyman's Horse Biting Him

The steed bit his master;
   How came this to pass?
He heard the good pastor
   Cry, 'All flesh is grass.'

Anon

# The National Union of Children

NUC has just passed a weighty resolution:
'Unless all parents raise our rate of pay
This action will be taken by our members
(The resolution comes in force today):—


'Noses will not be blown (sniffs are in order),
Bedtime will get preposterously late,
Ice-cream and crisps will be consumed for breakfast,
Unwanted cabbage left upon the plate,


'Earholes and finger-nails can't be inspected,
Overtime (known as homework) won't be worked,
Reports from school will all say "Could do better",
Putting bricks back in boxes may be shirked.'

*Roy Fuller*

# The National Association of Parents

Of course, NAP's answer quickly was forthcoming
(It was a matter of emergency),
It issued to the Press the following statement
(Its Secretary appeared upon TV):—

'True that the so-called Saturday allowance
Hasn't kept pace with prices in the shops,
But neither have, alas, parental wages:
NUC's claim would ruin kind, hard-working Pops.

'Therefore, unless that claim is now abandoned,
Strike action for us, too, is what remains;
In planning for the which we are in process
Of issuing, to all our members, canes.'

*Roy Fuller*

# The Mad Gardener's Song

He thought he saw an Elephant,
    That practised on a fife:
He looked again, and found it was
    A letter from his wife.
'At length I realise,' he said,
    'The bitterness of Life!'

He thought he saw a Buffalo
    Upon the chimney-piece:
He looked again, and found it was
    His Sister's Husband's Niece,
'Unless you leave this house,' he said,
    'I'll send for the Police!'

He thought he saw a Rattlesnake
    That questioned him in Greek:
He looked again, and found it was
    The Middle of Next Week.
'The one thing I regret,' he said,
    'Is that it cannot speak!'

He thought he saw a Banker's Clerk
    Descending from the 'bus:
He looked again, and found it was
    A Hippopotamus.
'If this should stay to dine,' he said,
    'There won't be much for us!'

He thought he saw a Kangaroo
    That worked a coffee-mill:

He looked again, and found it was
    A Vegetable-Pill.
'Were I to swallow this,' he said,
    'I should be very ill!'

He thought he saw a Coach-and-Four
    That stood beside his bed:
He looked again, and found it was
    A Bear without a Head.
'Poor thing,' he said, 'poor silly thing!
    It's waiting to be fed!'

He thought he saw an Albatross
    That fluttered round the lamp:
He looked again, and found it was
    A Penny-Postage-Stamp.
'You'd best be getting home,' he said,
    'The nights are very damp!'

He thought he saw a Garden-Door
    That opened with a key:
He looked again, and found it was
    A Double Rule of Three:
'And all its mystery,' he said,
    'Is clear as day to me!'

He thought he saw an Argument
    That proved he was the Pope:
He looked again, and found it was
    A Bar of Mottled Soap.
'A fact so dread,' he faintly said,
    'Extinguishes all hope!'

*Lewis Carroll*

# archy the cockroach is shocked

speaking of shocking things
and as so many people are these days
i noted an incident
in a subway train recently
that made my blood run cold
a dignified looking
gentleman with a long
brown beard
in an absent minded manner
suddenly reached up and
pulled his own left eye
from the socket and ate it

the consternation in the car
may be magined
people drew away from him
on all sides women screamed and
fainted in a moment every one
but the guard and myself
were huddled in the end of the car
looking at the dignified
gentleman with terror
the guard was sweating
with excitement but he stood
his ground sir said the guard
you cannot intimidate me
nor can you mystify me
i am a wise boid
you sir are a glass eater

and that was a glass eye
to the devil with a country
where people can t mind their own
business said the dignified
gentleman i am not a glass eater
if you must know and that was not
a glass eye it was a pickled onion
can not a man eat pickled
onions in this community
without exciting remark
the curse of this nation
is the number of meddlesome
matties
who are forever attempting
to restrict the liberty
of the individual i suppose
the next thing will be a law
on the statute books prohibiting
the consumption of pickled onions
and with another curse
he passed from the train
which had just then drawn up
beside
a station and went out
of my life forever

archy
*Don Marquis*

# The Belle of the Ball Room

Years—years ago—ere yet my dreams
  Had been of being wise or witty,—
Ere I had done with writing themes,
  Or yawn'd o'er this infernal Chitty;—
Years—years ago,—while all my joy
  Was in my fowling piece and filly,—
In short, while I was yet a boy,
  I fell in love with Laura Lily.


I saw her at the County Ball:
  There, when the sounds of flute and fiddle
Gave signal sweet in that old hall
  Of hands across and down the middle,
Hers was the subtlest spell by far
  Of all that set young hearts romancing;
She was our queen, our rose, our star;
  And then she danced—O Heaven, her dancing


Dark was her hair, her hand was white;
  Her voice was exquisitely tender;
Her eyes were full of liquid light;
  I never saw a waist so slender!
Her every look, her every smile,
  Shot right and left a score of arrows;
I thought 'twas Venus from her isle,
  And wonder'd where she'd left her sparrows.

She talk'd,—of politics or prayers,—
　　Of Southey's prose, or Wordsworth's sonnets,—
Of danglers—or of dancing bears,
　　Of battles—or the last new bonnets,
By candlelight, at twelve o'clock,
　　To me it mattered not a tittle;
If those bright lips had quoted Locke,
　　I might have thought they murmur'd Little.

Through sunny May, through sultry June,
　　I loved her with a love eternal;
I spoke her praises to the moon,
　　I wrote them to the Sunday Journal:
My mother laugh'd; I soon found out
　　That ancient ladies have no feeling:
My father frown'd; but how should gout
　　See any happiness in kneeling?

She was the daughter of a Dean,
　　Rich, fat, and rather apoplectic;
She had one brother, just thirteen,
　　Whose colour was extremely hectic;
Her grandmother for many a year
　　Had fed the parish with her bounty;
Her second cousin was a peer,
　　And Lord Lieutenant of the County.

But titles and the three per cents.,
　　And mortgages, and great relations,
And India bonds, and tithes, and rents,
　　Oh what are they to love's sensations?

Black eyes, fair forehead, clustering locks—
    Such wealth, such honours, Cupid chooses;
He cares as little for the Stocks
    As Baron Rothschild for the Muses.

She sketch'd; the vale, the wood, the beech,
    Grew lovelier from her pencil's shading:
She botanized; I envied each
    Young blossom in her boudoir fading:
She warbled Handel; it was grand;
    She made the Catalani jealous:
She touch'd the organ; I could stand
    For hours and hours to blow the bellows.

She kept an album, too, at home,
    Well fill'd with all an album's glories;
Paintings of butterflies, and Rome,
    Patterns for trimmings, Persian stories;
Soft songs to Julia's cockatoo,
    Fierce odes to Famine and to Slaughter,
And autographs of Prince Leboo,
    And recipes for elder-water.

And she was flatter'd, worshipp'd, bored;
    Her steps were watch'd, her dress was noted;
Her poodle dog was quite adored,
    Her sayings were extremely quoted;
She laugh'd and every heart was glad,
    As if the taxes were abolish'd;
She frown'd, and every look was sad,
    As if the Opera were demolish'd.

She smiled on many, just for fun,—
    I knew that there was nothing in it;
I was the first—the only one
    Her heart had thought of for a minute.—
I knew it, for she told me so,
    In phrase which was divinely moulded;
She wrote a charming hand,—and oh!
    How sweetly all her notes were folded!

Our love was like most other loves;—
    A little glow, a little shiver,
A rose-bud, and a pair of gloves,
    And 'Fly not yet'—upon the river;
Some jealousy of some-one's heir,
    Some hopes of dying broken hearted,
A miniature, a lock of hair,
    The usual vows,—and then we parted.

We parted; months and years roll'd by;
    We met again four summers after:
Our parting was all sob and sigh;
    Our meeting was all mirth and laughter:
For in my heart's most secret cell
    There had been many other lodgers;
And she was not the ball-room's Belle,
    But only—Mrs Something Rogers!
                    *W. M. Praed*

# More Anonymous
# Limericks

A diner while dining at Crewe
Found a rather large mouse in his stew.
    Said the waiter, 'Don't shout
    And wave it about,
Or the rest will be wanting one, too.'


A wonderful bird is the pelican,
His mouth can hold more than his belican,
    He can take in his beak
    Enough food for a week—
I'm damned if I know how the helican.


There was a young lady of Riga
Who went for a ride on a tiger:
    They returned from the ride
    With the lady inside
And a smile on the face of the tiger.


There was a faith-healer of Deal,
Who said, 'Although pain isn't real,
    If I sit on a pin
    And it punctures my skin,
I dislike what I fancy I feel.'

# Matilda

*Who told Lies, and was Burned to Death.*

Matilda told such Dreadful Lies,

It made one Gasp and Stretch one's Eyes;
Her Aunt, who, from her Earliest Youth,
Had kept a Strict Regard for Truth,

Attempted to Believe Matilda:
The effort very nearly killed her,
And would have done so, had not She
Discovered this Infirmity.
For once, towards the Close of Day,
Matilda, growing tired of play,

And finding she was left alone,
Went tiptoe

to

the Telephone
And summoned the Immediate Aid
Of London's Noble Fire-Brigade.
Within an hour the Gallant Band
Were pouring in on every hand,
From Putney, Hackney Downs and Bow,
With Courage high and Hearts a-glow
They galloped, roaring through the Town,

'Matilda's House is Burning Down!'
Inspired by British Cheers and Loud
Proceeding from the Frenzied Crowd,
They ran their ladders through a score
Of windows on the Ball Room Floor;
And took Peculiar Pains to Souse
The Pictures up and down the House,

Until Matilda's Aunt succeeded
In showing them they were not needed
And even then she had to pay
To get the Men to go away!

  .      .      .      .      .

It happened that a few Weeks later
Her Aunt was off to the Theatre
To see that Interesting Play

She had refused to take her Niece
To hear this Entertaining Piece:
A Deprivation Just and Wise
To Punish her for Telling Lies.
That Night a Fire *did* break out—
You should have heard Matilda Shout!
You should have heard her Scream and Bawl

And throw the window up and call
To People passing in the Street—
(The rapidly increasing Heat
Encouraging her to obtain
Their confidence)—but all in vain!
For every time She shouted 'Fire!'

They only answered 'Little Liar!'
And therefore when her Aunt returned,

# Matilda, and the House, were Burned.

*H. Belloc*

# The Signifying Monkey

The Monkey and the Lion
Got to talking one day.
Monkey looked down and said, 'Lion,
I hear you're king in every way.
But I know somebody
Who do not think that is true—
He told me he could whip
The living daylights out of you.'
Lion said, 'Who?'
Monkey said, 'Lion,
He talked about your mama
And talked about your grandma, too,
And I'm too polite to tell you
What he said about you.'
Lion said, 'Who said what? Who?'
Monkey in the tree,
Lion on the ground.
Monkey kept on signifying
But he didn't come down.
Monkey said, 'His name is Elephant—
He stone sure is not your friend.'
Lion said, 'He don't need to be
Because today will be his end.'
Lion took off through the jungle
Lickity-split,
Meaning to grab Elephant
And tear him bit to bit. Full stop!
He came across Elephant copping a righteous nod
Under a fine cool shady tree.

Lion said, 'You big old no-good so-and-so,
It's either you or me.'
Lion let out a solid roar
And bopped Elephant with his paw.
Elephant just took his trunk
And busted old Lion's jaw.
Lion let out another roar,
Reared up six feet tall.
Elephant just kicked him in the belly
And laughed to see him drop and fall.
Lion rolled over,
Copped Elephant by the throat.
Elephant just shook him loose
And butted him like a goat,
Then he tromped him and he stomped him
Till the Lion yelled, 'Oh, no!'
And it was near-nigh sunset
When Elephant let Lion go.
The signifying Monkey
Was still sitting in his tree
When he looked down and saw the Lion.
Said, 'Why, Lion, who can that there be?'
Lion said, 'Monkey, I don't want
To hear your jive-end jive.'
Monkey just kept on signifying,
'Lion, you for sure caught hell—
Mister Elephant's whipped you
To a fare-thee-well!
You ain't no king to me.
Fact is, I don't think that you
Can even as much as roar—

And if you try I'm liable
To come down out of this tree and
Whip your tail some more.'
The Monkey started laughing
And jumping up and down.
But he jumped so hard the limb broke
And he landed—bam!—on the ground.
When he went to run, his foot slipped
And he fell flat down.
Grrr-rrr-rr-r! The Lion was on him
With his front feet and his hind.
Monkey hollered, 'Ow!
I didn't mean it, Mister Lion!'
Lion said, 'You little flea-bag you!
Why, I'll eat you up alive.
I wouldn't a-been in this fix a-tall
Wasn't for your signifying jive.'
'*Please*,' said Monkey, 'Mister Lion,
If you'll just let me go,
I got something to tell you, please,
I think you ought to know.'
Lion let the Monkey loose
To see what his tale could be—
And Monkey jumped right back on up
Into his tree.
'What I was gonna tell you,' said Monkey,
'Is you square old so-and-so,
If you fool with me I'll get
Elephant to whip your head some more.'
'Monkey,' said the Lion,
Beat to his unbooted knees,

'You and all your signifying children
Better stay up in them trees.'
Which is why today
Monkey does his signifying
A-way-up out of the way.

*Traditional American*


# The Fleas

Great fleas have little fleas upon their backs to bite
    'em,
And little fleas have lesser fleas and so ad infinitum.
And the great fleas themselves, in turn, have greater
    fleas to go on;
While these again have greater still, and greater still,
    and so on.

*A. De Morgan*


# The Termite

Some primal termite knocked on wood
And tasted it, and found it good;
And that is why your Cousin May
Fell through the parlour floor today.

*Ogden Nash*

# Little Billee

There were three sailors of Bristol city
Who took a boat and went to sea.
But first with beef and captain's biscuits
And pickled pork they loaded she.

There was gorging Jack and guzzling Jimmy,
And the youngest he was little Billee.
Now when they got as far as the Equator
They'd nothing left but one split pea.

Says gorging Jack to guzzling Jimmy,
'I am extremely hungaree.'
To gorging Jack says guzzling Jimmy,
'We've nothing left, us must eat we.'

Says gorging Jack to guzzling Jimmy,
'With one another we shouldn't agree!
There's little Bill, he's young and tender,
We're old and tough, so let's eat he.'

'Oh! Billy, we're going to kill and eat you,
So undo the buttons of your chemie.'
When Bill received this information
He used his pocket handkerchie.

'First let me say my catechism,
Which my poor mammy taught to me.'
'Make haste, make haste,' says guzzling Jimmy,
While Jack pulled out his snickersnee.

So Billy went up to the main-top gallant mast,
And down he fell on his bended knee.
He scarce had come to the twelfth commandment
When up he jumps, 'There's land I see:

'Jerusalem and Madagascar,
And North and South Amerikee:
There's the British flag a-riding at anchor,
With Admiral Napier, K.C.B.'

So when they got aboard of the Admiral's,
He hanged fat Jack and flogged Jimmee;
But as for little Bill he made him
The Captain of a Seventy-three.

W. M. Thackeray

# The Common Cormorant

The common cormorant or shag
Lays eggs inside a paper bag
The reason you will see no doubt
It is to keep the lightning out.
But what these unobservant birds
Have never noticed is that herds
Of wandering bears may come with buns
And steal the bags to hold the crumbs.

*Anon*

# Bees

Every bee
that
ever was
was
partly
sting
and partly
. . . buzz.

*Jack Prelutsky*

# Why Nobody Pets the Lion
## at the Zoo

The morning that the world began
The Lion growled a growl at Man.

And I suspect the Lion might
(If he'd been closer) have tried a bite.

I think that's as it ought to be
And not as it was taught to me.

I think the Lion has a right
To growl a growl and bite a bite.

And if the Lion bothered Adam,
He should have growled right back at 'im.

The way to treat a Lion right
Is growl for growl and bite for bite.

True, the Lion is better fit
For biting than for being bit.

But if you look him in the eye
You'll find the Lion's rather shy.

He really wants someone to pet him.
The trouble is: his teeth won't let him.

He has a heart of gold beneath
But the Lion just can't trust his teeth.

*John Ciardi*

# My Brother Bert

Pets are the Hobby of my brother Bert.
He used to go to school with a Mouse in his shirt.

His Hobby it grew, as some hobbies will,
And grew and GREW and GREW until—

Oh don't breathe a word, pretend you haven't heard.
A simply appalling thing has occurred—

The very thought makes me iller and iller:
Bert's brought home a gigantic Gorilla!

If you think that's really not such a scare,
What if it quarrels with his Grizzly Bear?

You still think you could keep your head?
What if the Lion from under the bed

And the four Ostriches that deposit
Their football eggs in his bedroom closet

And the Aardvark out of his bottom drawer
All danced out and joined in the Roar?

What if the Pangolins were to caper
Out of their nests behind the wallpaper?

With the fifty sorts of Bats
That hang on his hatstand like old hats,

And out of a shoebox the excitable Platypus
Along with the Ocelot or Jungle-Cattypus?

The Wombat, the Dingo, the Gecko, the Grampus—
How they would shake the house with their Rumpus!

Not to forget the Bandicoot
Who would certainly peer from his battered old boot.

Why it could be a dreadful day,
And what Oh what would the neighbours say!

*Ted Hughes*

# Percy the Pest

Percy was a liar,
Percy was a pest.
So they bought a one-way ticket
And packed him off to Jest—
Where many a true word is spoken.

*Grimsdyke Churchforest*

# The Rolling English Road

Before the Roman came to Rye or out to Severn
strode,
The rolling English drunkard made the rolling
English road.
A reeling road, a rolling road, that rambles round
the shire,
And after him the parson ran, the sexton and the
squire;
A merry road, a mazy road, and such as we did tread
The night we went to Birmingham by way of Beachy
Head.

I knew no harm of Bonaparte and plenty of the
Squire,
And for to fight the Frenchman I did not much
desire;
But I did bash their baggonets because they came
arrayed
To straighten out the crooked road an English
drunkard made,
Where you and I went down the lane with ale-mugs
in our hands,
The night we went to Glastonbury by way of Good-
win Sands.

His sins they were forgiven him; or why do flowers
run
Behind him, and the hedges all strengthening in the
sun?

The wild thing went from left to right and knew not
    which was which,
But the wild rose was above him when they found
    him in the ditch.
God pardon us, nor harden us; we did not see so clear
The night we went to Bannockburn by way of
    Brighton Pier.

My friends, we will not go again or ape an ancient
    rage,
Or stretch the folly of our youth to be the shame of
    age,
But walk with clearer eyes and ears this path that
    wandereth,
And see undrugged in evening light the decent inn
    of death;
For there is good news yet to hear and fine things to
    be seen,
Before we go to Paradise by way of Kensal Green.
G. K. Chesterton

# Eaper Weaper

Eaper Weaper, chimbley-sweeper,
Had a wife but couldn't keep her,
Had annover, didn't lover her,
Up the chimbley he did shover.
Anon

# The Akond of Swat

Who or why, or which, or *what*,
          Is the Akond of SWAT?

Is he tall or short, or dark or fair?
Does he sit on a stool or a sofa or chair,   or SQUAT,
          The Akond of Swat?

Is he wise or foolish, young or old?
Does he drink his soup and his coffee cold,   or HOT,
          The Akond of Swat?

Does he sing or whistle, jabber or talk,
And when riding abroad does he gallop or walk,   or
    TROT,
          The Akond of Swat?

Does he wear a turban, a fez, or a hat?
Does he sleep on a mattress, a bed, or a mat,   or a
    COT,
          The Akond of Swat?

When he writes a copy in round-hand size,
Does he cross his T's and finish his I's,   with a DOT,
          The Akond of Swat?

Can he write a letter concisely clear
Without a speck or a smudge or smear,   or BLOT,
          The Akond of Swat?

Do his people like him extremely well?
Or do they, whenever they can, rebel,   or PLOT,
　　　　　　At the Akond of Swat?

If he catches them then, either old or young,
Does he have them chopped in pieces or hung,   or
　SHOT,
　　　　　　The Akond of Swat?

Do his people prig in the lanes or park?
Or even at times, when days are dark,   GAROTTE?
　　　　　　O the Akond of Swat?

Does he study the wants of his own dominion?
Or doesn't he care for public opinion,   a JOT,
　　　　　　The Akond of Swat?

To amuse his mind do his people show him
Pictures, or any one's last new poem,   or WHAT,
　　　　　　For the Akond of Swat?

At night if he suddenly screams and wakes,
Do they bring him only a few small cakes,   or a LOT,
　　　　　　For the Akond of Swat?

Does he live on turnips, tea, or tripe?
Does he like his shawl to be marked with a stripe,
　or a DOT,
　　　　　　The Akond of Swat?

Does he like to lie on his back in a boat
Like the lady who lived in that isle remote,
   SHALLOTT,
                 The Akond of Swat?

Is he quiet, or always making a fuss?
Is his steward a Swiss or a Swede or a Russ,   or a
   SCOT,
                 The Akond of Swat?

Does he like to sit by the calm blue wave?
Or to sleep and snore in a dark green cave,   or a
   GROT,
                 The Akond of Swat?

Does he drink small beer from a silver jug?
Or a bowl? or a glass? or a cup? or a mug?   or a
   POT
                 The Akond of Swat?

Does he beat his wife with a gold-topped pipe,
When she lets the gooseberries grow too ripe,   or
   ROT,
                 The Akond of Swat?

Does he wear a white tie when he dines with friends,
And tie it neat in a bow with ends,   or a KNOT,
                 The Akond of Swat?

Does he like new cream, and hate mince-pies?
When he looks at the sun does he wink his eyes,   or
     NOT,
                    The Akond of Swat?

Does he teach his subjects to roast and bake?
Does he sail about on an inland lake,   in a YACHT,
                    The Akond of Swat?

Some one, or nobody, knows I wot
Who or which or why or what
                    Is the Akond of Swat!

*Edward Lear*


# The Man in the Wilderness

The man in the wilderness asked of me,
How many strawberries grow in the sea?
I answered him as I thought good,
As many red herrings as grow in the wood.

*Anon*

# The Shooting of Dan McGrew

A bunch of the boys were whooping it up in the
    Malamute saloon;
The kid that handles the music-box was hitting a
    rag-time tune;
Back of the bar, in a solo game, sat Dangerous Dan
    McGrew,
And watching his luck was his light-o'-love, the lady
    that's known as Lou.

When out of the night, which was fifty below, and
    into the din and the glare,
There stumbled a miner fresh from the creeks, dog-
    dirty and loaded for bear.
He looked like a man with a foot in the grave, and
    scarcely the strength of a louse,
Yet he tilted a poke of dust on the bar, and he called
    for drinks for the house.
There was none could place the stranger's face,
    though we searched ourselves for a clue;
But we drank his health, and the last to drink was
    Dangerous Dan McGrew.

There's men that somehow just grip your eyes, and
    hold them hard like a spell;
And such was he, and he looked to me like a man
    who had lived in hell;
With a face most hair, and the dreary stare of a dog
    whose day is done,
As he watered the green stuff in his glass, and the
    drops fell one by one.

Then I got to figgering who he was, and wondering
    what he'd do,
And I turned my head—and there watching him
    was the lady that's known as Lou.

His eyes went rubbering round the room, and he
    seemed in a kind of daze,
Till at last that old piano fell in the way of his
    wandering gaze.
The rag-time kid was having a drink; there was no
    one else on the stool,
So the stranger stumbles across the room, and flops
    down there like a fool.
In a buckskin shirt that was glazed with dirt he sat,
    and I saw him sway;
Then he clutched the keys with his talon hands—
    my God! but that man could play!

Were you ever out in the Great Alone, when the
    moon was awful clear,
And the icy mountains hemmed you in with a silence
    you most could *hear*;
With only the howl of a timber wolf, and you camped
    there in the cold,
A half-dead thing in a stark, dead world, clean mad
    for the muck called gold;
While high overhead, green, yellow, and red, the
    North Light swept in bars—
Then you've a haunch what the music meant . . .
    hunger and night and the stars.

And hunger not of the belly kind, that's banished
    with bacon and beans;
But the gnawing hunger of lonely men for a home and
    all that it means;
For a fireside far from the cares that are, four walls
    and a roof above;
But oh! so cramful of cosy joy, and crowned with a
    woman's love:
A woman dearer than all the world, and true as
    Heaven is true—
(God! how ghastly she looks through her rouge,—
    the lady that's known as Lou.)


Then on a sudden the music changed, so soft that
    you scarce could hear;
But you felt that your life had been looted clean of
    all that it once held dear;
That someone had stolen the woman you loved; that
    her love was a devil's lie;
That your guts were gone, and the best for you was
    to crawl away and die.
'Twas the crowning cry of a heart's despair, and it
    thrilled you through and through—
'I guess I'll make it a spread misère,' said Dangerous
    Dan McGrew.


The music almost died away ... then it burst like a
    pent-up flood;

And it seemed to say, 'Repay, repay,' and my eyes
    were blind with blood.
The thought came back of an ancient wrong, and it
    stung like a frozen lash,
And the lust awoke to kill, to kill . . . then the music
    stopped with a crash.

And the stranger turned, and his eyes they burned
    in a most peculiar way;
In a buckskin shirt that was glazed with dirt he sat,
    and I saw him sway;
Then his lips went in in a kind of grin, and he spoke,
    and his voice was calm;
And, 'Boys,' says he, 'you don't know me, and none
    of you care a damn;
But I want to state, and my words are straight, and
    I'll bet my poke they're true,
That one of you is a hound of hell . . . and that one
    is Dan McGrew.'

Then I ducked my head, and the lights went out,
    and two guns blazed in the dark;
And a woman screamed, and the lights went up, and
    two men lay stiff and stark.
Pitched on his head, and pumped full of lead, was
    Dangerous Dan McGrew,
While the man from the creeks lay clutched to the
    breast of the lady that's known as Lou.

These are the simple facts of the case, and I guess I
  ought to know,
They say that the stranger was crazed with 'hooch',
  and I'm not denying it's so.
I'm not so wise as the lawyer guys, but strictly
  between us two—
The woman that kissed him—and pinched his poke—
  was the lady that's known as Lou.

*Robert Service*


# The Walrus

The Walrus lives on icy floes
And unsuspecting Eskimoes.

Don't bring your wife to Arctic Tundra
A Walrus may bob up from undra.

*Michael Flanders*

# The Llama

The Llama is a woolly sort of fleecy hairy goat,
With an indolent expression and an undulating
    throat
  Like an unsuccessful literary man.

And I know the place he lives in (or at least—
    I think I do)
It is Ecuador, Brazil or Chili—possibly Peru;
    You must find it in the Atlas if you can.

The Llama of the Pampasses you never should
   confound
(In spite of a deceptive similarity of sound)
   With the Lhama who is Lord of Turkestan.

For the former is a beautiful and valuable
      beast,
But the latter is not lovable nor useful in the
      least;
And the Ruminant is preferable surely to the
      Priest
Who battens on the woeful superstitions of the
      East,
   The Mongol of the Monastery of Shan.

*H. Belloc*

# King Foo Foo

King Foo Foo sat upon his throne
Dressed in his royal closes,
While all round his courtiers stood
With clothes-pegs on their noses.

'This action strange,' King Foo Foo said,
'My mind quite discomposes,
Though vulgar curiosity
A good king never shoses.'

But to the court it was as clear
As poetry or prose is:
King Foo Foo had not had a bath
Since goodness only knowses.

But one fine day the Fire Brigade
Rehearsing with their hoses
(To Handel's 'Water Music' played
With many puffs and bloses.)

Quite failed the water to control
In all its ebbs and floses
And simply drenched the King with sev-
Eral thousand gallon doses.

At this each wight (though impolite)
A mighty grin exposes.
'At last,' the King said, 'now I see
That all my court morose is!

'A debt to keep his courtiers gay
A monarch surely owses,
And deep within my royal breast
A sporting heart reposes.'

So now each night its water bright
The Fire Brigade disposes
Over a King who smiles as sweet
As all the royal roses.

*Charles Causley*


# Gasbags

I'm thankful that the sun and moon
Are both hung up so high
That no pretentious hand can stretch
And pull them from the sky.
If they were not, I have no doubt,
But some reforming ass
Would recommend to take them down
And light the world with gas.

*Anon: Nineteenth Century*

# A Dromedary Standing Still

A dromedary standing still
resembles stilts beneath a hill,
and when he lopes along the ground
he seems to be a walking mound.

A herd observed from far away
in lumpy, bumpy disarray
appears to be a very strange
perambulating mountain range.

*Jack Prelutsky*

# The Armadillo

The ancient armadillo
is as simple as the rain,
he's an armour-plated pillow
with a microscopic brain.

He's disinterested thoroughly
in what the world has wrought,
but spends his time in contemplative,
armadyllic thought.

*Jack Prelutsky*

# Mr Kartoffel

Mr Kartoffel's a whimsical man;
He drinks his beer from a watering can,
And for no good reason that I can see
He fills his pockets with china tea.
He parts his hair with a knife and fork
And takes his ducks for a Sunday walk.
Says he, 'If my wife and I should choose
To wear our stockings outside our shoes,
Plant tulip bulbs in the baby's pram
And eat tobacco instead of jam
And fill the bath with cauliflowers,
That's nobody's business at all but ours.'
Says Mrs K., 'I may choose to travel
With a sack of grass or a sack of gravel,
Or paint my toes, one black, one white,
Or sit on a bird's nest half the night—
But whatever I do that is rum or rare,
I rather think that it's my affair.
So fill up your pockets with stamps and string,
And let us be ready for anything!'
Says Mr K. to his whimsical wife,
'How can we face the storms of life,
Unless we are ready for anything?
So if you've provided the stamps and string,
Let us pump up the saddle and harness the horse
And fill him with carrots and custard and sauce,
Let us leap on him lightly and give him a shove
And it's over the sea and away, my love!'

James Reeves

# The Walrus and the Carpenter

The sun was shining on the sea,
　　Shining with all its might:
He did his very best to make
　　The billows smooth and bright—
And this was odd, because it was
　　The middle of the night.

The moon was shining sulkily,
　　Because she thought the sun
Had got no business to be there
　　After the day was done—
'It's very rude of him,' she said,
　　'To come and spoil the fun!'

The sea was wet as wet could be,
　　The sands were dry as dry.
You could not see a cloud, because
　　No cloud was in the sky:
No birds were flying overhead—
　　There were no birds to fly.

The Walrus and the Carpenter
　　Were walking close at hand;
They wept like anything to see
　　Such quantities of sand:
'If this were only cleared away,'
　　They said, 'it *would* be grand!'

'If seven maids with seven mops
  Swept it for half a year,
Do you suppose,' the Walrus said,
  'That they could get it clear?'
'I doubt it,' said the Carpenter,
  And shed a bitter tear.

'O Oysters, come and walk with us!'
  The Walrus did beseech.
'A pleasant walk, a pleasant talk,
  Along the briny beach:
We cannot do with more than four,
  To give a hand to each.'

The eldest Oyster looked at him,
  But never a word he said:
The eldest Oyster winked his eye,

And shook his heavy head—
Meaning to say he did not choose
    To leave the oyster-bed.

But four young oysters hurried up,
    All eager for the treat:
Their coats were brushed, their faces washed,
    Their shoes were clean and neat—
And this was odd, because, you know,
    They hadn't any feet.

Four other Oysters followed them,
    And yet another four;
And thick and fast they came at last,
    And more, and more, and more—
All hopping through the frothy waves,
    And scrambling to the shore.

The Walrus and the Carpenter
    Walked on a mile or so,
And then they rested on a rock
    Conveniently low:
And all the little Oysters stood
    And waited in a row.

'The time has come,' the Walrus said,
    'To talk of many things:
Of shoes—and ships—and sealing-wax—
    Of cabbages—and kings—
And why the sea is boiling hot—
    And whether pigs have wings.'

'But wait a bit,' the Oysters cried,
  'Before we have our chat;
For some of us are out of breath,
  And all of us are fat!'
'No hurry!' said the Carpenter.
  They thanked him much for that.

'A loaf of bread,' the Walrus said,
  'Is what we chiefly need:
Pepper and vinegar besides
  Are very good indeed—
Now if you're ready, Oysters dear,
  We can begin to feed.'

'But not on us!' the Oysters cried,
  Turning a little blue,

'After such kindness, that would be
    A dismal thing to do!'
'The night is fine,' the Walrus said.
    'Do you admire the view?

'It was so kind of you to come!
    And you are very nice!'
The Carpenter said nothing but
    'Cut us another slice:
I wish you were not quite so deaf—
    I've had to ask you twice!'

'It seems a shame,' the Walrus said,
    'To play them such a trick.
After we've brought them out so far,
    And made them trot so quick!'
The Carpenter said nothing but
    'The butter's spread too thick!'

'I weep for you,' the Walrus said,
  'I deeply sympathize.'
With sobs and tears he sorted out
  Those of the largest size,
Holding his pocket-handkerchief
  Before his streaming eyes.

'O Oysters,' said the Carpenter.
  'You've had a pleasant run!
Shall we be trotting home again?'
  But answer came there none—
And this was scarcely odd, because
  They'd eaten every one.

*Lewis Carroll*


# Manners

I eat my peas with honey
I've done it all my life
It makes the peas taste funny
But it keeps 'em on the knife!

*Anon*

# Lovey-Dovey

Poets call the dove
The symbol of pure love;
But have you heard the things they do?
COO!

*Harold Morland*

# Springtime

'Tis dog's delight to bark and bite
And little birds to sing,
And if you sit on a red-hot brick
It's a sign of an early spring.

*Anon*

# The Rain

The rain it raineth every day,
  Upon the just and unjust fellow,
But more upon the just, because
  The unjust hath the just's umbrella.

*Anon*

# The Hob-Nailed Boots what Farver Wore

My farver's feet filled up arf a street
So his boots was in proportion,
And the kids he'd squash in a week, by gosh!
It really was a caution.
Well, me and me bruvvers at the age of four,
All wrapped up cosy in a box of straw,
Till eleven in the morning used to sleep and snore,
In the hob-nailed boots what farver wore.

When Madge and Flo went to Southend, so
As money they'd be saving
Father's boots were seen as a bathin' machine
Where the bathers 'ud change for bathin'.
Well, while they was changin', they forgot, I'm sure,
The hole he had cut for his corns, and cor!
The boys started giggling at what they saw—
In the hob-nailed boots what farver wore.

Now, we had a goat with a cast iron throat,
Though she never used to bite us;
She died one Sunday in the afternoon
Of acute appendicitis.
Now, she had whiskers used to touch the floor
And when they was plaited by the kids next door
They made the finest laces that you ever saw
For the hob-nailed boots what farver wore.

When I went to school, well, I felt a fool,
For one day when we was drillin',
The teacher said, 'Toe the line fathead',
And I did that most unwillin'.
She said, 'I'll-tell-you-and-I've-told-you-before,
Don't keep backin' through the schoolhouse door.
'Well, just toe the line!' said the kids with a roar,
'In the hob-nailed boots what farver wore.'

On the Lord Mayor's day just to shout hoorah,
Father went and how he sauced 'em;
But his plates of meat stuck across the street
So the Lord Mayor drove across them.
As he was going through the Guildhall door
Father fell flat across his back and swore,
And the crowd started booing then, 'cos all they saw
Was the hob-nailed boots what farver wore.

*Traditional English*

# The Hunter

The hunter crouches in his blind
'Neath camouflage of every kind,
And conjures up a quacking noise
To lend allure to his decoys.
This grown-up man, with pluck and luck,
Is hoping to outwit a duck.

*Ogden Nash*

# The Pessimist

Nothing to do but work,
  Nothing to eat but food,
Nothing to wear but clothes,
  To keep one from going nude.

Nothing to breathe but air,
  Quick as a flash 'tis gone;
Nowhere to fall but off,
  Nowhere to stand but on.

Nothing to comb but hair,
  Nowhere to sleep but in bed,
Nothing to weep but tears,
  Nothing to bury but dead.

Nothing to sing but songs,
  Ah, well, alas! alack!
Nowhere to go but out,
  Nowhere to come but back.

Nothing to see but sights,
  Nothing to quench but thirst,
Nothing to have but what we've got,
  Thus through life we are cursed.

Nothing to strike but a gait;
  Everything moves that goes.
Nothing at all but common sense
  Can ever withstand these woes.

*Ben King*

# More Limericks of Edward Lear

There was a Young Lady of Portugal,
Whose ideas were excessively nautical:
  She climbed up a tree,
  To examine the sea,
But declared she would never leave Portugal.

There was an old man of Blackheath,
Whose head was adorned with a wreath,
Of lobsters and spice, pickled onions and mice,
That uncommon old man of Blackheath.

# Mungojerrie and Rumpelteazer

Mungojerrie and Rumpelteazer were a very notori-
ous couple of cats.
As knockabout clowns, quick-change comedians,
tight-rope walkers and acrobats
They had an extensive reputation. They made their
home in Victoria Grove—
That was merely their centre of operation, for they
were incurably given to rove.
They were very well known in Cornwall Gardens, in
Launceston Place and in Kensington Square—
They had really a little more reputation than a
couple of cats can very well bear.


If the area window was found ajar
And the basement looked like a field of war,
If a tile or two came loose on the roof,
Which presently ceased to be waterproof,
If the drawers were pulled out from the bedroom
chests,
And you couldn't find one of your winter vests,
Or after supper one of the girls
Suddenly missed her Woolworth pearls:
Then the family would say: 'It's that horrible cat!
It was Mungojerrie—or Rumpelteazer!'—And most
of the time they left it at that.

Mungojerrie and Rumpelteazer had a very unusual
   gift of the gab.
They were highly efficient cat-burglars as well, and
   remarkably smart at a smash-and-grab.
They made their home in Victoria Grove. They had
   no regular occupation.
They were plausible fellows, and liked to engage a
   friendly policeman in conversation.

When the family assembled for Sunday dinner,
With their minds made up that they wouldn't
   get thinner
On Argentine joint, potatoes and greens,
And the cook would appear from behind the
   scenes
And say in a voice that was broken with sorrow:
'I'm afraid you must wait and have dinner
   *tomorrow*!
For the joint has gone from the oven—like that!'
Then the family would say: 'It's that horrible cat!
It was Mungojerrie—or Rumpelteazer!'—And most
   of the time they left it at that.

Mungojerrie and Rumpelteazer had a wonderful
   way of working together.
And some of the time you would say it was luck, and
   some of the time you would say it was weather.
They would go through the house like a hurricane,
   and no sober person could take his oath
Was it Mungojerrie—or Rumpelteazer? or could you
   have sworn that it mightn't be both?

And when you heard a dining-room smash
Or up from the pantry there came a loud crash
Or down from the library came a loud *ping*
From a vase which was commonly said to be
Ming—
Then the family would say: 'Now which was which
cat?
It was Mungojerrie! AND Rumpelteazer!'—And
there's nothing at all to be done about that!

*T. S. Eliot*


# The Despairing Lover

Distracted with care
For Phyllis the fair,
Since nothing could move her,
Poor Damon, her lover,
Resolves in despair
No longer to languish,
Nor bear so much anguish:
But, mad with his love,
To a precipice goes,
Where a leap from above
Would soon finish his woes.

When in rage he came there,
Beholding how steep
The sides did appear,
And the bottom how deep;

His torments projecting,
And sadly reflecting,
That a lover forsaken
A new love may get,
But a neck, when once broken,
Can never be set:
And, that he could die
Whenever he would,
But, that he could live
But as long as he could:
How grievous soever
The torment might grow,
He scorn'd to endeavour
To finish it so.
But bold, unconcern'd
At thoughts of the pain,
He calmly return'd
To his cottage again.

*William Walsh*


# Swans Sing Before They Die

Swans sing before they die—'twere no bad thing
Should certain persons die before they sing.

*S. T. Coleridge*

# Mr Timothy Pringle

Mr Timothy Pringle
Lived on his own
As he was single.
Returning from work
In the evening gloom
He found an elephant
In his room.
It had a label
Round its neck
'My name is Doris
Eileen Beck'.
Even if the name was Jim
It didn't really help poor Tim.
Is that elephant a her or he?
Asked Mrs Screws (the landlady)
Tim said 'It's a female elephant, why?'
'No women in rooms' was the stern reply.

*Spike Milligan*


# Marriage

When a man has married a wife he finds out whether
Her knees and elbows are only glued together.

*William Blake*

# More Ruthless Rhymes
## of Harry Graham

## Aunt

Aunt, a most delightful soul
But with little self-control,
    When run over by a 'taxi',
    Grew unconscionably waxy.

She could not have made more fuss
Had it been a motor-bus!

## Billy

Billy, in one of his nice new sashes,
    Fell in the fire and was burned to ashes;
Now, although the room grows chilly,
    I haven't the heart to poke poor Billy.

## London Calling

When rabies attacked my Uncle Daniel,
And he had fits of barking like a spaniel,
The B.B.C. relayed him (from all stations)
At *Children's Hour* in 'farmyard imitations'.

# The World Has Held Great Heroes

The world has held great Heroes,
  As history books have showed;
But never a name to go down to fame
  Compared with that of Toad!

The clever men at Oxford
  Know all there is to be knowed.
But they none of them know one half as much
  As intelligent Mr Toad!

The animals sat in the Ark and cried,
  Their tears in torrents flowed.
Who was it said 'There's land ahead'?
  Encouraging Mr Toad!

The Army all saluted
  As they marched along the road.
Was it the King? Or Kitchener?
  No. It was Mr Toad!

The Queen and her Ladies in waiting
  Sat at the window and sewed.
She cried: 'Look! who's that handsome man?'
  They answered: 'Mr Toad.'

The motor-car went Poop-poop-poop,
  As it raced along the road,
Who was it steered it into a pond?
  Ingenious Mr Toad.

*Kenneth Grahame*

# artists shouldnt have offspring

*(A bulletin from Archy the Cockroach, who started out last July to hitch-hike from Hollywood to New York with Mehitabel the Cat and Mehitabel's seven platinum-blonde kittens)*

had a great ride boss
got a ride on the running board of a car
and caught up with mehitabel
in new mexico where she is gadding about
with a coyote friend
i asked her where the kittens were
kittens said mehitabel kittens
with a puzzled look on her face
why goodness gracious i seem to remember
that i did have some kittens
i hope nothing terrible has happened
to the poor little things but if something has
i suppose they are better off
an artist like me shouldnt really
have offspring it handicaps her career
archy i want you to meet my boy friend
cowboy bill the coyote i call him
i am trying to get him to come to new york
with me and do a burlesque turn
isnt he handsome i said tactfully that he looked
very distinguished to me and all bill said
was nerts insect nerts

> archy

*Don Marquis*

# The Giraffe

The Giraffe is tall,
Looks down on us all,

Lofty, stiff-necked,
Lip curled, erect,

With humourless eye
Looks down from on high,

Gives a curt little nod,
Says, 'I'm nearer to God.'

He's his own High Horse,
Can't get down, of course.
*Michael Flanders*


# The Camel

Man with his hydro-electric power
Has learnt to make the desert flower,
A pleasing change to every mammal —
Except the desert-loving Camel.

He sees, with mounting irritation,
The ravages of irrigation
And water, as it flows and squirts,
Deprive him of his just desserts.
*Michael Flanders*

# The Sailor's Consolation

One night came on a hurricane,
    The sea was mountains rolling,
When Barney Buntline slewed his quid
    And said to Billy Bowline:
'A strong nor'-wester's blowing, Bill:
    Hark: don't ye hear it roar now?
Lord help 'em, how I pities them
    Unhappy folks on shore now.


'Foolhardy chaps as live in towns,
    What danger they are all in,
And now lie quaking in their beds,
    For fear the roof should fall in!
Poor creatures, how they envies us
    And wishes, I've a notion,
For our good luck in such a storm
    To be upon the ocean!


'And as for them that's out all day
    On business from their houses,
And late at night returning home
    To cheer their babes and spouses;
While you and I, Bill, on the deck
    Are comfortably lying,
My eyes! what tiles and chimney-pots
    About their heads are flying!

'Both you and I have oft-times heard
  How men are killed and undone
By overturns from carriages,
  By thieves and fires, in London.
We know what risks these landsmen run,
  From noblemen to tailors;
Then, Bill, let us thank Providence
  That you and I are sailors.'

Charles Dibdin

# Routine

No matter what we are and who,
Some duties everyone must do:

A Poet puts aside his wreath
To wash his face and brush his teeth,

And even Earls
Must comb their curls,

And even Kings
Have underthings.

Arthur Guiterman

# You are Old, Father William

'You are old, Father William,' the young man said,
  'And your hair has become very white;
And yet you incessantly stand on your head—
  Do you think, at your age, it is right?'

'In my youth,' Father William replied to his son,
  'I feared it might injure the brain;
But, now that I'm perfectly sure I have none,
  Why, I do it again and again.'

'You are old,' said the youth, 'as I mentioned before,
   And have grown most uncommonly fat;
Yet you turned a back-somersault in at the door—
   Pray, what is the reason for that?'

'In my youth,' said the sage, as he shook his grey
     locks,
   'I kept all my limbs very supple
By the use of this ointment—one shilling the box—
   Allow me to sell you a couple?'

'You are old,' said the youth, 'and your jaws are too
weak
  For anything tougher than suet;
Yet you finished the goose, with the bones and the
beak—
  Pray, how did you manage to do it?'

'In my youth,' said his father, 'I took to the law,
  And argued each case with my wife;
And the muscular strength, which it gave to my jaw,
  Has lasted the rest of my life.'

'You are old,' said the youth, 'one would hardly suppose
    That your eye was as steady as ever;
Yet you balance an eel on the end of your nose—
    What made you so awfully clever?'

'I have answered three questions, and that is enough,'
    Said his father; 'don't give yourself airs!
Do you think I can listen all day to such stuff?
    Be off, or I'll kick you downstairs!'

*Lewis Carroll*

# Acknowledgements

The Editor gratefully acknowledges permission to reprint copyright material to the following:

Gerald Duckworth & Co. Ltd. for *The Python, The Big Baboon, Matilda,* and *The Llama,* from 'Cautionary Verses' by H. Belloc; John Murray (Publishers) Ltd. for *Hunter Trials* from 'Collected Poems' by John Betjeman; David Higham Associates Ltd. for *King Foo Foo* from 'Figgie Hobbin' by Charles Causley, published by Macmillan; A. P. Watt & Son and Miss D. E. Collins and Methuen & Co. for *The Rolling English Road* from 'The Collected Poems' of G. K. Chesterton'; Wm. Collins Sons & Co. Ltd. for *The Sad Demise of Sally Point-Toe Jane* and *Percy the Pest* by Grimsdyke Churchforest; John Ciardi for *Why Nobody Pets the Lion at the Zoo*; MacGibbon & Kee for *nobody loses all the time* from 'Complete Poems' by e e cummings; Faber and Faber Ltd. for *Growltiger's Last Stand* and *Mungojerrie and Rumpelteazer* from 'Old Possum's Book of Practical Cats' by T. S. Eliot; Dennis Dobson, publishers for *The Walrus, The Camel,* and *The Giraffe* from 'Creatures Great and Small' by Michael Flanders; André Deutsch Ltd. for *Ermyntrude, The National Union of Children,* and *The National Association of Parents* from 'Seen Grandpa Lately?' by Roy Fuller; Edward Arnold (Publishers) Ltd. for the selection of *Ruthless Rhymes* by Harry Graham; The Bodleian Library, Oxford, and Methuen & Co. Ltd. for *The World Has Held Great Heroes* from 'The Wind in the Willows' by Kenneth Grahame; The Society of Authors as the literary representative of the Estate of A. E. Housman, and Jonathan Cape Ltd., publishers of *A.E.H.* by Laurence Housman for *Inhuman Henry*; Faber and Faber Ltd. for *My Brother Bert* from 'Meet My Folks' by Ted Hughes; Faber and Faber Ltd. for *archy is shocked* from 'Archy & Mehitabel' and *artists shouldnt have offspring* from 'Archy's Life of Mehitabel' by Don Marquis; Spike Milligan for *The Terns* and *Mr Timothy Pringle*; J. M. Dent & Sons Ltd. for *The Hunter* from 'Versus' and for *The Termite* from 'Family Reunion', and André Deutsch Ltd. for *Next* from 'Bedriddance' by Ogden Nash; Hamish Hamilton for *Bees, A Dromedary,* and *The Armadillo* from 'Zoo Doings and Other Poems' by Jack Prelutsky; William Heinemann Ltd. for *Mr Kartoffel* from 'The Wandering Moon' by James Reeves; Ernest Benn Ltd. for *The Shooting of Dan McGrew* from 'Collected Poems' by Robert Service.

Every effort has been made to trace the owners of the copyright material in this book. It is the Editor's belief that all necessary permissions have been obtained, but in the case of any question arising as to the use of any material, the Editor will be pleased to make the necessary correction in future editions of the book.